CONTENTS

T0346213

INTRODUCTION

"This is the news. Due to a computer error this morning, jetcars on the north skyway face a three-hour delay. Two people are in the hospital after their hoverbike came crashing to the ground. On the bright side, the city's weather-control computer is fixed, so the rest of the day will be warm and sunny. Fly safely!"

In the future we may travel almost everywhere by air. Science and technology will give us new kinds of aircraft, from jetpacks worn by one person, to buses that float around cities.

... and awesome racing planes.

But new technology is only part of the story. How will we make air transport safe and organised in the future? What about fuel use, pollution and the environment? There are many challenges to overcome to make air travel the best way to get around.

... futuristic choppers ...

... super-fast personal jetpacks ...

TAKING OFF

Compared to travel by land and sea, air transport has only just started. The first aeroplane flew just over 100 years ago. Since then people have developed all kinds of aircraft, from small helicopters to giant jumbo jets carrying more than 800 people.

PLANES TAKE OFF

Wilbur and Orville Wright flew the first proper aeroplane on 17th December 1903. It was called the Wright Flyer. During the First World War (1914–1918) countries began to develop new kinds of aeroplanes for fighting and spying. By the 1930s, air travel was a popular way to move post, passengers and goods from place to place.

*Steam-powered aeroplanes were tried out in the 1930s. But the fuel, such as coal, was too heavy to carry enough for a long flight. It was also difficult to feed smoothly into the boiler, to keep the **propellers** spinning. Liquid fuels were the way forwards.*

The Wright Flyer III carried the first air passenger in 1908.

TAKING SHAPE

Engineers tried out different aircraft designs, such as "flying wings". The Junkers G.38 flew for the first time in 1929. It carried over 30 people, including six in each wing! Flying wings are still designed today (see page 11).

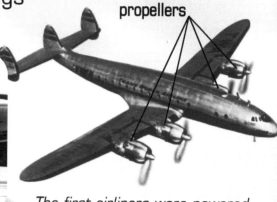

propellers

The Junkers G.38 flew for the first time in 1929.

The first airliners were powered by propeller engines, like this Lockheed Constellation.

The airship Hindenburg exploded in New Jersey, USA, killing 35 people.

AIR DISASTER

Not every new invention caught on. Airships are huge balloons that float in the sky, carrying passengers underneath. They were once a popular way to travel from Europe to the USA. After the airship Hindenburg exploded in 1937, people did not want to travel by airship any more.

FLYING HIGH

Today, most aeroplanes share a similar shape: a long body, two large wings, a **tailplane** and a tail fin. The basic design has changed little, though many different ideas have been tried.

In the 1960s, the Aviation Traders Carvair tried to compete with car ferries. It flew up to five cars and 20 passengers in less than half the time of a ferry service. Twenty-one Carvairs were built, but eight crashed and tickets were very expensive.

PUSHING THE LIMITS

In the mid-1900s, aeroplane designers tried out lots of new ideas. Aeroplanes were designed to meet every need, from taking a car on holiday, to a "flying car" that could be kept at home! But there were many problems. It soon became clear that flying was not the best way to travel short distances, or to carry very heavy loads.

This early flying car is made from a car and a small aeroplane fixed together! It was too heavy to take off.

N100D

tail fin

tailplane

wing

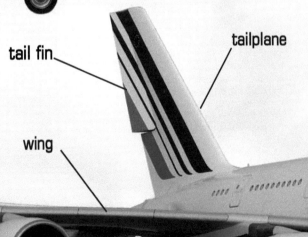

jet engine

The giant Airbus A380 first flew in 2005. It has a "double deck" that can seat more than 800 people.

FLYING FASTER

Today, most large aeroplanes are powered by **jet engines**, instead of propellers. Jet planes first flew in the Second World War (1939–45). The technology was first used in passenger planes in the 1950s. Today's jet planes fly faster and further, using less fuel.

From 1976, Concorde planes flew passengers across the Atlantic Ocean at speeds faster than sound. There was a terrible crash in 2000, and in 2003 the Concorde planes stopped flying.

Boeing's 787 Dreamliner can fly very long distances. It is built from light, strong materials to save fuel. It first flew in 2009.

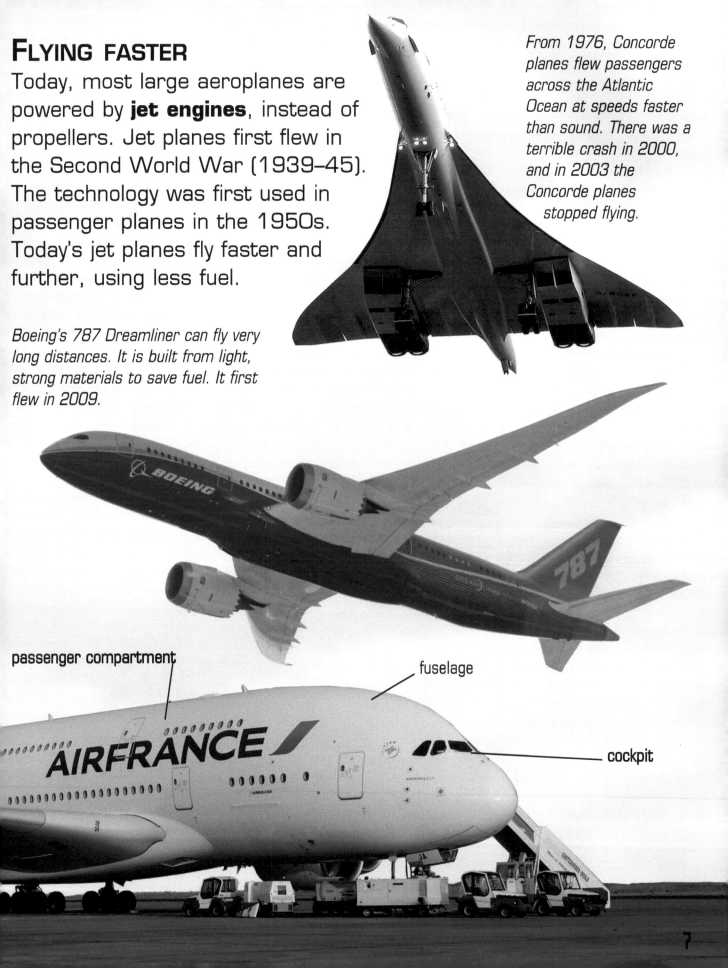

passenger compartment

fuselage

cockpit

FUTURE AIRLINERS

Airliners are large planes, designed to carry many passengers at once. Future airliners will need to meet the demand for speedy, comfortable journeys. They will also need to be energy-efficient with low pollution.

Companies such as Boeing are testing different airliner designs, to see which might be best for future planes.

PLANE SAILING

One way to make airliners more efficient is to change the shape of the wings. Long, narrow wings have a greater lifting force. They allow the plane to "sail" through the air like a glider, using less engine power. This trick is already used by long-winged birds, like the albatross!

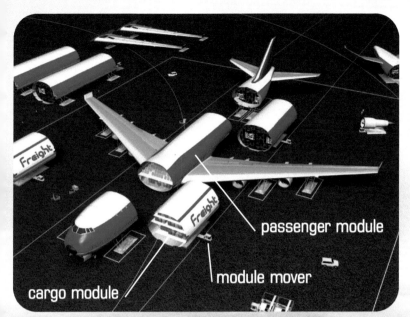

passenger module

module mover

cargo module

Modular airliners?

Loading and unloading **cargo** or passengers takes time and so costs money. Future airliners may split into "modules" that can be loaded quickly. They are joined back together when it is time to take off.

Eco flyers

We have eco-friendly electric cars and electric trains, so why not electric planes? Today's batteries are too heavy and bulky to get off the ground. In the future, lighter batteries could be recharged as a plane flies.

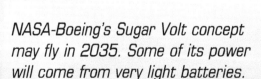

NASA-Boeing's Sugar Volt concept may fly in 2035. Some of its power will come from very light batteries.

LIGHT PLANES

Some of the most exciting future air travel ideas are for light planes that can be used like family cars. They would have to be big enough to carry a family and their luggage on holiday, but small enough to fly into cities on shopping trips.

The Terrafugia Transition fits in an average garage when its wings are folded. On the road, it can reach speeds of 105 kilometres per hour. In the air, it can cruise at 172 kilometres per hour.

COMBI FLY-DRIVES

Some futuristic light planes will be designed for flying only. Others may be combinations of car and aeroplane, boat and aeroplane, or all three! They will need to take off and land quickly, in a space no longer than a driveway. They must be **stable** in the air and simple to control, so everyone can be a pilot.

*The ultra-light Samba is like a flying motorcycle. It is a combination of light plane and **microlight**.*

Icon A5 Amphibious Sportsplane

Pilots who don't live near a landing strip could use a nearby lake or river. The Icon A5 is a two-person microlight that can land on water or solid ground. The first Icon A5 made its test flight in 2008. It will be sold for around £90,000.

Icon A5 in flight

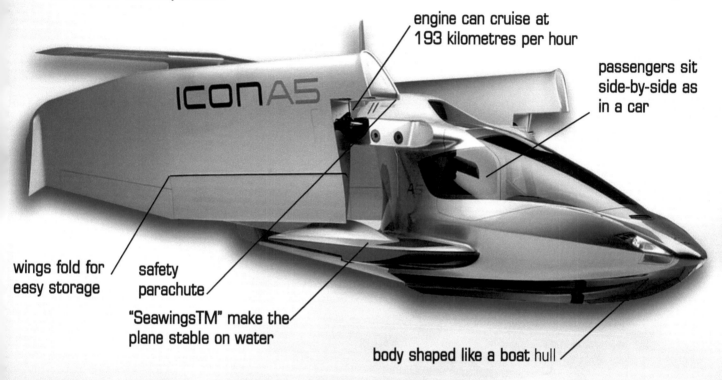

engine can cruise at 193 kilometres per hour

passengers sit side-by-side as in a car

wings fold for easy storage

safety parachute

"SeawingsTM" make the plane stable on water

body shaped like a boat hull

This two-seater Electravia ElectroClub would be powered by an electric motor that is almost silent.

Next Big Step?

Light planes of the future may be based on the Blended Wing Body (BWB) or "flying wing" design (see page 5). The large wing area provides plenty of **lift**. This means they use much less fuel – and fly more quietly – than helicopters. Some BWBs are easily blown about by strong winds, so designers are trying to make them more stable.

WHIRLYBIRDS

Helicopters are like cars for the sky. They are so convenient and useful! But they are also expensive to buy, costly to keep and tricky to fly.

Igarashi Design's SNOC idea seats just one person, like a motorcycle for the sky.

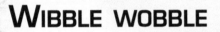

WIBBLE WOBBLE

Helicopters wobble in the air so they need skilled pilots to stop them tumbling out of the sky. Their blades have to be carefully looked after and they burn huge amounts of fuel.

Kocyba have designed a "Bumblebee" helicopter with two sets of blades that fold up on landing. It could be useful as an air taxi!

The new Eurocopter X3 has two engines that spin both the main rotor and two side-by-side rotors to boost its speed.

IN A SPIN

As a helicopter's main blades spin one way, its body tries to turn the other way. This is why most helicopters have a smaller **rotor** at the back. Another solution is to have two sets of blades one above the other but spinning different ways.

blades

fan

tyres for road driving

AVX's TX design changes from car to helicopter in just one minute! When it wants to take off, two sets of blades fold out and connect to the engine, lifting the TX into the sky. Fans at the back push it along in the sky or on the ground.

The fans of this "Verticopter" point down to take off vertically like a helicopter. In the air, they tilt backwards to push the aircraft along like a plane.

QUICK JETS

Planes that travel faster than sound have been around since 1947, when US test pilot Chuck Yeager broke the "sound barrier" in his Bell X-1 rocket plane. However, at the moment there are no passenger planes that travel this fast. Going **supersonic** is a challenge for aircraft designers of the future.

*An F-15 Eagle creates a **shock wave** as it breaks the sound barrier.*

*A supersonic airliner idea from Lockheed Martin has engines on top of the wings. This should quieten the **sonic boom** when going faster than sound, which disturbs people on the ground.*

SUPER SLEEK

Supersonic planes need a long, slim, **streamlined** shape with a pointed nose and tail. This helps the plane to push through the air. At speeds faster than sound, normal plane designs cause huge drag and give a very uncomfortable ride.

The BAE Taranis is an idea for a robot fighter plane. A future version may be able to travel at almost twice the speed of sound.

SONIC CRUISERS

The only supersonic passenger craft was Concorde, which flew from 1976 to 2003. People loved its graceful shape, but it was noisy, and used a lot of fuel. New supersonic passenger jets will need to be quiet and efficient.

The ultra-rich like to be one step ahead. Supersonic business jets, like this Aerion design, would allow them to fly from London to New York for a meeting, and return the same day!

CHANGING SHAPE

Supersonic airliners will be slimmer than today's airliners, but longer so they can still fit many passengers on board. Windows cause problems at high speeds, so will probably be left out of future designs. Passengers will have to watch films and play games instead of looking at the view.

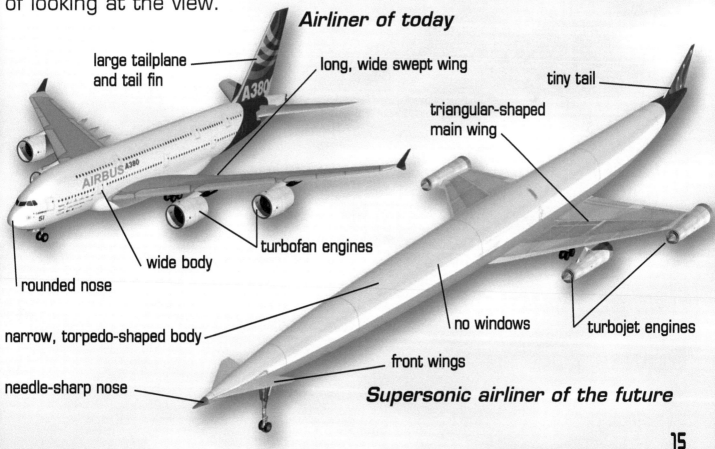

Airliner of today

large tailplane and tail fin

long, wide swept wing

tiny tail

triangular-shaped main wing

turbofan engines

wide body

rounded nose

narrow, torpedo-shaped body

no windows

turbojet engines

front wings

needle-sharp nose

Supersonic airliner of the future

GROUND EFFECT

Keeping a large plane high in the sky uses lots of energy and fuel. In the future, some journeys may be made in Ground-Effect Vehicles (GEVs). They skim along just above the water – or the land!

SEA SKIMMERS

In one way, the GEV is like a hovercraft. It flies just a few metres above the water. The air flowing down from under the wings pushes against the surface of the water and keeps the plane up. This cushion of air means that less energy is needed to keep the craft airborne, so it can carry bigger loads with smaller engines and less fuel. The problem comes when high winds and storms whip up big waves.

The Aquaglide 5 is a small GEV. It can carry five people at a flight speed of 170 kilometres per hour or a water speed of 88 kilometres per hour.

Small GEVs are called flarecraft or flareboats, like the SeaFalcon (above). They are great for having fun on the water. Their short wings give just enough lift to skate 1.5 to 3 metres above the surface.

The Beriev Be-2500 Neptun is the largest aircraft ever designed. If built, it would be over 150 metres long and weigh more than 2,000 metric tons. It could cruise along just above the water, like a flying ship, or fly at 9,000 metres.

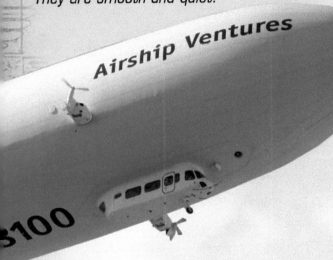

Modern airships like the AV ZNT are used when people need to take photographs or films from the air. They are smooth and quiet.

LIGHTER THAN AIR

During the 1930s, airships were known as the "queens of the skies". They flew thousands of people in enormous luxury. But several fires, explosions and bad-weather disasters ended the airship's rule. Can new technology help them return?

GOOD AND BAD

Airships are filled with gases that are lighter than air, such as helium. This gives them their lift.

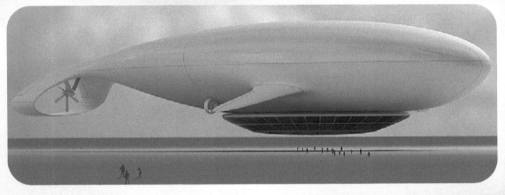

Imagine a flying hotel that circled the world in a few days. The Manned Cloud design could carry 40 passengers.

They are energy efficient because they only need to burn fuel to make them go forwards. But a flight may be against the wind, which is where difficulties begin. Rough weather means these giant "gas-bags" have to hide in **hangars**.

This "spy airship" is being tested by the US military. At 76 metres long, it could stay in the sky for up to 3 weeks, taking photographs.

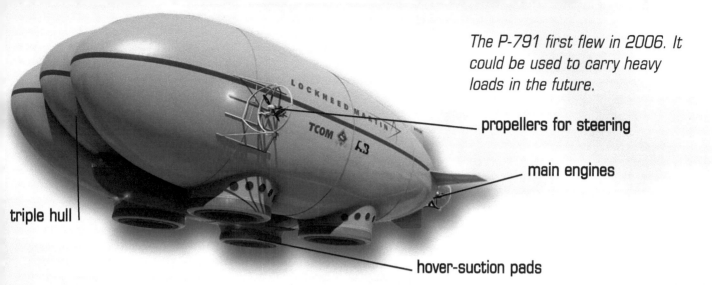

The P-791 first flew in 2006. It could be used to carry heavy loads in the future.

propellers for steering

main engines

triple hull

hover-suction pads

CARGO BUSTERS

Passengers dislike bad weather delays. But airships could carry huge loads of non-urgent cargo to remote areas without airfields. The next challenge is how to balance the airship as it picks up or drops off heavy loads. Powerful pumps may be needed to move the gases inside and keep the ship stable.

This Aeroscraft airship design has mini wings to give it extra lift and control. It is powered by solar panels covering the top of its huge body.

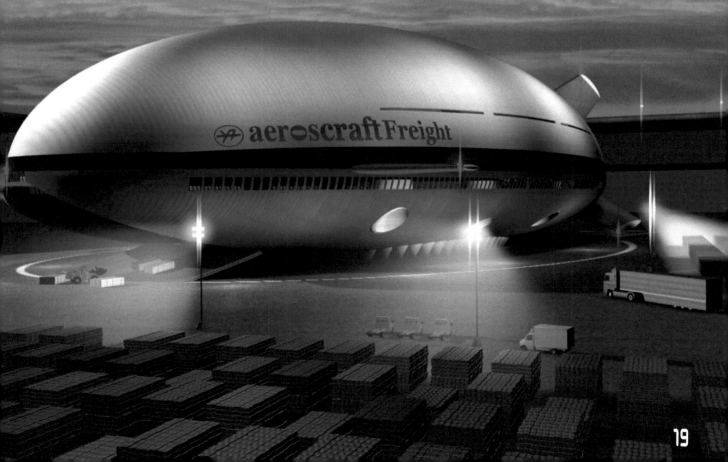

PERSONAL FLIGHT

Many people dream of strapping on a backpack and zooming off into the sky. Personal flight may look awesome, but if things go wrong, you can only blame the pilot!

In 2008 Yves Rossy crossed the English Channel with his rocket-wing. He has had several near-misses and some hard landings, too.

Many kinds of jetpacks, like this rocket belt, have been tested over the years. But a wrong twitch of the controls can lead to disaster.

HIGH POWERED

There are several ways of powering one-person flight. They include small helicopter blades, mini-jets, baby rockets and blasts of compressed gas. With powerful machinery at the pilot's back or side, danger is truly just around the corner. But for some, the feeling of freedom is worth the risk.

The Martin Jetpack works using "jets" of air from two fans driven by a lightweight engine. After test flights in 2008, its controls are now being improved.

PERSONAL SPACE INVADERS

Jetpack flying needs huge care. It is difficult to see what's behind – or above, below and even to the sides. In the future, pilots may wear a special headset with a display that shows them what is nearby. Jetpacks may even steer themselves, to avoid bumps or crashes.

Boots, backpacks, pods and wings might be used for different kinds of flying trips.

AERO POWER

Most air transport relies on jets, propellers and the occasional rocket. Will a new kind of power take over in years to come?

REVOLUTION IN THE AIR

Propellers and jet engines rely on moving parts. These can break down easily, and be damaged if they hit objects in the air, such as flocks of birds. Future engines may overcome this problem by having fewer moving parts.

PulseJet Racer's engines will have no moving parts. They suck in air, burn it and send blasts of gas shooting out of the back to push the plane forwards.

This is the huge jet engine from a modern airliner. Its massive fan is taller than a man.

This ultra-light plane has four battery-powered electric motors.

AIRBORNE ALTERNATIVES

If future batteries weigh less and last longer, then the electric plane could be the next big step. Even better would be solar panels on an aeroplane's wings, to turn free sunlight into electricity to power the motors. But batteries would still be needed for cloudy weather and night flights.

Solar Impulse has huge wings over 61 metres across, yet carries just one person. The wings are covered with solar panels to charge the batteries that power the propellers.

These jets have fan-like blades on the outside. They use less fuel than normal jets, but they are slow and noisy. They could be used for cheap, short flights.

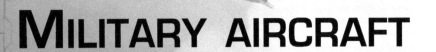

MILITARY AIRCRAFT

The US X-47B will be able to spy and fight without a pilot on board!

Air power is not just about speed, guns and bombs. Future warplanes will be controlled by computers so smart, they may not even need pilots!

SHHHH! STEALTH

A stealth plane can carry out missions without the enemy knowing. The plane's special shape and surface stop it from being picked up by **radar**. Its hot engine exhaust gases are cooled and spread out, so the plane cannot be spotted by heat detectors either. The planes even fly more quietly than normal planes!

Stealth planes like the F-117 Nighthawk (below) have specially-shaped wings.

UNMANNED PLANES

"Robot planes" have no pilots. They can fly near enemies without putting a crew in danger. Some are remote-controlled from the ground. The latest designs can be programmed with a mission. Clever computers on board decide how to carry out the mission.

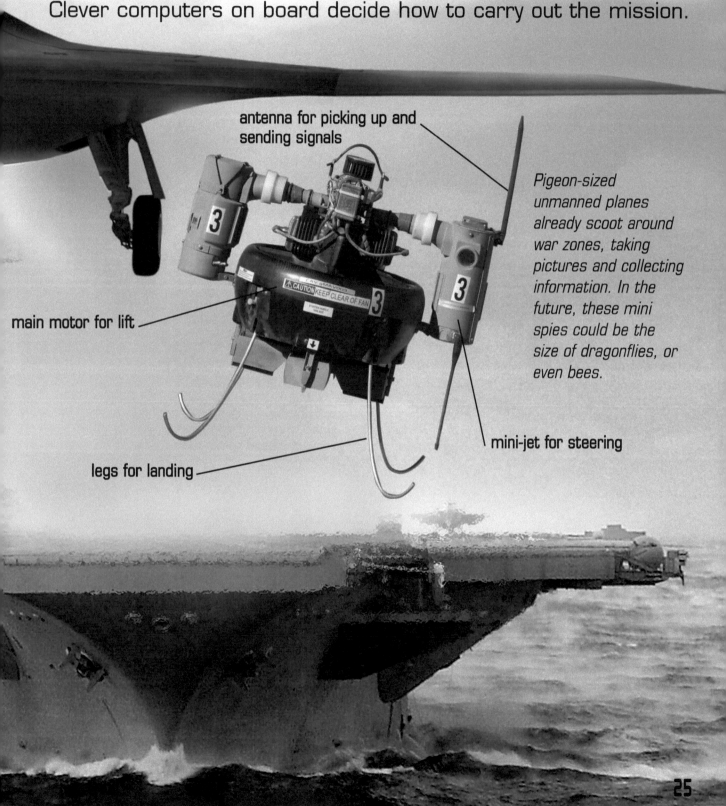

antenna for picking up and sending signals

main motor for lift

legs for landing

mini-jet for steering

Pigeon-sized unmanned planes already scoot around war zones, taking pictures and collecting information. In the future, these mini spies could be the size of dragonflies, or even bees.

AIR SAFETY

Air transport is not only the fastest way to travel, it's also one of the safest. New technology will reduce risks even more, as aircraft get smarter and airports become more secure.

As passengers pass through security checks, the system builds up a complete picture of their behaviour.

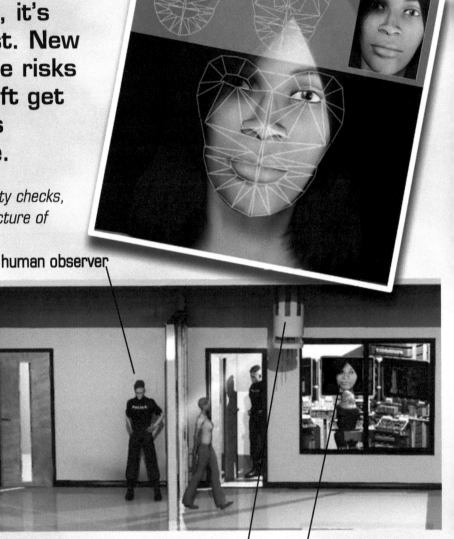

facial recognition readout

human observer

body temperature check

full body scanner

camera checks movements

eye scanner

SECURITY CHECKS

In the future, airport security won't just check what passengers are carrying. Cameras and **sensors** will check everyone's body movements and temperature, face, breathing and eyes. This alerts staff to people who seem nervous or are acting strangely before they reach the plane.

IN THE AIR

Sadly, accidents can happen. Aeroplanes of the future will be designed to reduce the risks at every stage of the flight. This includes building back-up systems in case the main ones fail. The newest planes even have back-up systems that back up the back-ups!

"Black box" flight recorders are usually orange, so they can be easily found after an accident.

DESIGN AND TRAINING

After an air accident, experts check the aeroplane's "black box" flight recorder to find out what went wrong and why. The black box records the crew's voices, and the readings from the aeroplane's instruments. This information will help planes and pilots of the future to be safer than ever before.

In the future, planes may even be able to change their shape to cope with emergencies such as bad weather. This is called "Refuse to Crash" technology.

Pilots spend many hours each year training on the ground! Inside a flight simulator, they learn how to react to a huge range of problems, from thick fog to an engine fire.

FUTURE AIRPORTS

Aircraft of the future will be faster, safer, more comfortable and less harmful to the environment. What about airports? As air transport grows, they will have to cope with more passengers and cargo.

Future security scanners may work in "real time" so people are checked as they walk past, rather than waiting in queues. They will also see hidden weapons under clothing.

LESS WAITING TIME

Ticket, travel documents, passport, security, baggage check, body search ... airport passengers are soon worn out. Checks of the future will be quicker, because they will be based on biometrics. These are detailed body measurements, from a map of your eyes and face, to voice analysis. A computer will scan these things quickly, to check who every passenger is.

Airports often win awards for futuristic design, such as Incheon in South Korea.

In giant airports people have to walk a long way to get to the planes. In this new design, people park in the basement, check in just above, and take the escalator to the plane on top.

three side-by-side turbofan engines

Future planes like this "Double Bubble" will be designed for faster unloading and loading at airports. It is like two planes joined in the middle.

extra doors

GLOSSARY

CARGO
goods carried by a plane

FUSELAGE
main body of an aeroplane

HANGAR
large building for storing aeroplanes

HULL
main body of a ship or airship

JET ENGINE
engine that causes forward movement by the power of a stream of gases being forced out in the opposite direction

LIFT
upward force

MICROLIGHT
very small and light one- or two-seater aeroplane

PROPELLERS
rotating blades that make small aeroplanes move forward

RADAR
system that uses radio waves to find moving aircraft and ships

ROTOR
spinning blades of a helicopter

SENSORS
electrical devices that can detect movement or sound

SHOCK WAVE
huge travelling wave of pressure

SIMULATOR
ground-based machine that has an exact copy of an aeroplane's controls and can be used to practise flying in different types of weather

SONIC BOOM
explosive sound caused when an aeroplane travels faster than the speed of sound

STABLE
unlikely to overturn

STREAMLINED
designed to minimise air and water resistance

SUPERSONIC
faster than the speed of sound

TAILPLANE
a wing on a plane's tail

INDEX